The KETO Crockpot

40 scrumptious, simple, fat-burning, health-boosting recipes that cook themselves while you're on the go!

CARRIE BROWN

from

The Ketovangelist Kitchen

ISBN-13: 978-1545091395
ISBN-10: 1545091390

DEDICATION

Alisen Petersen

The woman with whom I share a brain. My best friend. My wing-woman.

You ran my errands, battled with real estate legalities, schlepped my a** to the coffee shop for a break every weekend, pored over my recipe collection categorizing them, washed dishes, polished silverware, and took Mr. McHenry outside so he could get his wiggles out...and that's just the start of your awesomeness.

All this so I could stay heads down on this cookbook without the rest of my world falling down around my ears while I was peering into numerous crock pots, shooting pictures of everything that sat on a plate long enough, and churning out more food than I could eat in 3 months.

On an ongoing basis you eat an endless stream of mystery food, cheer loudly and often, and come up with a bunch of brilliant ideas. I simply wouldn't do life nearly as well without you.

THANK YOU.

ACKNOWLEDGMENTS

Brian Williamson — I don't even know where to start. I am so incredibly grateful every. single. day. that you emailed me last summer, and for your continual, daily encouragement and support from the sidelines; oh, and for not yelling.
Let me just say YOU. ARE. AWESOME. and THANK YOU!

Rekka Jay — for your brilliant, arty, watermarking, logo-ing, social media-ing, book-cover-creating time and talents — THANK YOU!

Minta Hale — you get so very excited about everything I make, and the new recipes for this cookbook were no exception. For the daily food review texts after you'd eaten your dinner, and for offering to tackle the mountain of dishes — THANK YOU!

The Ketovangelist Kitchen Facebook Admin Crew — for your endless enthusiasm for what I do, for taking care of business when I need to disconnect and stay wrapped up in my apron, for your loud and raucous cheerleading, and for making me laugh with your shenanigans every single day — THANK YOU!

Marc Levine — it will always be you that I think about every morning when I get to wake up and enjoy another beautiful day — THANK YOU!

You — THANK YOU for being here, and for giving me the best reason to do what I do: help you reach your health and wellness goals.
If you bought this book, follow my blog, listen to our podcasts, or cheer from the sidelines on social media — THANK YOU. You are a very important part of my world and none of this would be worth it without you.

CONTENTS

THE ULTIMATE FAST FOOD (IN ONLY 6 – 8 HOURS!)

It's all kinds of an oxymoron to tell you that this cookbook is full of fast food when it actually takes 6 – 8 hours to cook, right? But what I really mean is that these recipes will allow you to walk in the door at the end of a long day and have dinner all ready and waiting for you.

The fastest way to getting dinner ready isn't grabbing packets of frozen food (or in a lot of cases 'edible products') and tossing them in your microwave when you roll in the house exhausted after a full day of doing. Nope, it's walking in, lifting the lid off your crockpot and scooping hot, delicious, nutritious food onto your plate. And that, lovely cooks, is the beauty of the crockpot.

Crockpot cooking is incredibly simple. There is nothing complicated or difficult or inherently different about crockpot cooking. It is simply an alternative vessel in which to get your food cooked. You can cook any crockpot recipe on the stovetop or in the oven, and many recipes can also be converted to work in a pressure cooker or Instant Pot. The only thing that is different between all these cooking devices is the different combinations of temperature and time used. So although these recipes were all developed for and in a crockpot, you should be able to cook them perfectly on the stovetop or in the oven, too. I've added a handy time and temperature conversion chart for you on page 6.

NOTE: Using these recipes as they are written, in a pressure cooker or Instant Pot isn't advised, as these appliances have specific needs in order to work. Many of the recipes would need to be adjusted. If you are a very seasoned pressure cooker or Instant Pot user then feel free to take a stab at converting them, but if you're not super-familiar with those appliances, I'd stick to using a crockpot, stovetop, or oven for the recipes contained herein.

So why crockpot if you can make all these recipes on the stovetop or in the oven in a fraction of the time? Because time. Huh? Despite the fact that crockpots typically take 6 – 8 hours to cook anything, the #1 reason why the crockpot is your best friend is because it is so hands-off, and does all the heavy lifting while you are away doing something else. When you use the stovetop or oven methods it's much more hands-on, and you need to hang around the kitchen. So while they may be faster all-up, the crockpot is the real rock star of the fast food show. You get to leave the kitchen – or better still – the house, and when you get back all you have to do is lift the lid, scoop out delicious food, and eat.

Having said that crockpot cooking is incredibly simple, there are still a few tips and tricks in the next chapter on using a crockpot that will help you get the best results.

When the chorus of voices requesting a KETO Crockpot Cookbook began reaching the level of deafening and I started to plan recipes, some requests came in over and over again. I was struck that you were asking for recipes that had minimal prep, and also minimal post-cooking work. Isn't crockpot cooking all about not much effort? I headed to The Internet to figure out why this was even a *thing,* and it turns out the majority of regular crockpot recipes I found have either significant pre-cooking or post-cooking effort required, or both; which seemed to negate the whole point of crockpot cooking. Many crockpot recipes out there are just way too long and complicated, and don't highlight the crockpot's best feature: reducing the time you spend in the kitchen cooking.

I also wondered why so many of you were clamoring for a specifically KETO Crockpot Cookbook at all. A meander around Pinterest helped me understand the need. So. Much. Carbage. in most regular crockpot recipes! Most regular crockpot recipes revolve around starchy foods, which makes them a no-go for all us low-carb folks.

Thus, my goals for this cookbook were set:

- Recipes that require minimal prep.
- Recipes that require minimal or zero post-cooking work.
- Recipes that don't revolve around starchy foods.
- One-pot recipes that can be eaten without the need for a separate side or accompaniment.
- Simple, whole-food ingredients available to most everyone, most everywhere.
- As few 'strange' ingredients as possible.
- Recipes that can be prepped ahead and frozen 'raw' and then thawed and crockpotted when needed.
- Recipes that can be made and cooked in bulk and successfully frozen in portions for eating in the future – further saving significant time and effort.
- Simple recipes that the least experienced cook can follow and get great results.
- All the basic tenants of KETO: no grains, gluten, sugars, starches, soy, or industrialized processed vegetable and seed oils.
- Ingredients that are very low- or no-carb, and / or are low on the glycemic index.
- Delicious recipes that no one will know were created for a 'special' diet or lifestyle.
- A large variety of recipes to save the time and frustration of searching for recipes online that you don't know will work, and don't know will be delicious.
- Budget-friendly recipes that are within reach of most households.

So that's what you can expect from the recipes in this cookbook. In an attempt to make this a useful cookbook for the most people, a few require a little more work than others, and a few include some lower-starch veggies for those that can tolerate them.

For dairy-intolerant folks, there are 30 recipes that are non-dairy as-is or have easy dairy subs, and 10 that would need significant recipe changes to make them dairy-free. The dairy-free or subbed recipes are noted in the index by "*". Subs are indicated in the recipe's ingredients lists.

Lastly, you will notice a two-letter designation in the corner of each recipe picture either CK (Certified Ketogenic), KA (Ketogenic Approved), or KF (Ketogenic Friendly). For information on what the designations signify, please head over to www.certifiedketogenic.com for full details.

And now, here's some tips and tricks to help you get your Keto Crockpot on!

CROCKPOT COOKING: TIPS AND TRICKS

Choosing a crockpot / slow cooker:

- If you don't have a crockpot, choose one with an automatic switch-off so that once the cooking time is over the crockpot switches to warm. That allows you to not be there at the end of cooking time, but keeps your food warm until you arrive, without over-cooking it.

    (See resources: http://carriebrown.com/keto-crockpot-resources-qa)

- The recipes in this cookbook were all made in a 6 quart crockpot or a 6 quart Instant Pot (on the crockpot setting), but you can get larger or smaller crockpots. I recommend getting one larger than you need so that you have more flexibility, and can also make the full recipes and freeze the leftovers if it's more than you need at the first sitting. Then you have another meal(s) ready that only require defrosting and reheating, saving you even more time. A larger crockpot also means you are less likely to overfill your crockpot – something that is not recommended. You don't want a crockpot too small that you then overfill it, since an overfilled crockpot will mean your food will steam instead of simmer. No Bueno.

- If you have a crockpot that does not have an automatic switch-off, get yourself a plug-in timer so that you can set the crockpot to switch on and off at specific times, meaning your food won't overcook if you are gone for longer than the cooking time.

    (See resources: http://carriebrown.com/keto-crockpot-resources-qa)

- You can also get a plug-in attachment that will switch your crockpot to warm after the cooking time has ended.
    (See resources: http://carriebrown.com/keto-crockpot-resources-qa)

- You can also get Wi-Fi enabled crockpots that you can control from your cell phone (!!). Switch them on, off, change the temperature setting, and switch them to warm, wherever you are. So if your plans change on the fly, dinner won't be ruined.

Preparing your crockpot:

- If you do not use crockpot liners, lightly spray the inside of your crockpot with coconut or avocado oil spray before putting your food in. This will make cleaning easier.

- For fast and easy clean-up use crockpot liners. Remove the food, toss the liner. Clean-up = done.

(See resources: http://carriebrown.com/keto-crockpot-resources-qa)

- Before you start preparing your ingredients for the crockpot, switch it on to pre-heat, unless you are preparing it earlier in the day to switch it on at a later time, e.g. If you have a Wi-Fi enabled crockpot or an automatic timer / plug in attachment.

Choosing and preparing your ingredients:

- Use fattier cuts of meat and dark-meat poultry to help ensure the moistest, most delicious results. Think short ribs, pork butt (shoulder), lamb shanks, rib roasts, back ribs, tri-tip. For poultry think thighs, legs, wings.

- Use bone-in cuts of meat as these will provide moister meat than boneless cuts. This applies especially to lower-fat cuts such as pork chops.

- Always use dried herbs. Fresh herbs are way too delicate for long-cooking methods and you will end up with no herb flavor. If you have an abundance of fresh herbs growing in your yard that you want to use up – or leftover fresh herbs from some other cooking project – then chop them and stir them into your dish once cooking is over and you are about to serve.

- A good rule of thumb is to chop all the main ingredients into similar-sized pieces to ensure even cooking. The exception to this would be when you are cooking a whole joint of meat with veggies.

- Place the longer-cooking foods on the bottom e.g. place the roast on top of your veggies. This ensures food at the bottom gets the most heat, and also protects the meat from scorching.

- Make sure all ingredients are fully thawed before adding to your crockpot. Adding frozen foods puts you at risk of eating improperly cooked food, and that rarely leads anywhere good.

- With meat you have 2 choices – to brown first or not. If you have the time to brown your meat before placing it in the crockpot you will enjoy a deeper, more flavorful end dish, and also a more attractive one. However, if you are in a time crunch you can add the meat un-browned and it will cook just fine. I **highly** recommend browning whenever you can. The boost to flavor and appearance is significant.

- If you are using skin-on chicken pieces then **always** brown first. Boiled chicken skin is extremely unattractive in both look and taste! Trust me on this one. The exception being if you smother it in something so wildly delicious you don't notice it. See page 53.

- If you are using ground meat then **always** brown first so that you can break up the meat, otherwise you will have a solid lump of meat at the end of the cooking time! It is also a lot more difficult to incorporate other ingredients into raw ground meat well.

- Only use konjac flour / glucomannan powder as your thickener. DO NOT try and swap it out with guar or xanthan gum. (See following chapter on konjac flour for details). Seriously, DO NOT SWAP OUT WITH GUMS.

- You can prep your ingredients and prepare your dish ahead, cooking it at a later time e.g. prep before you go to bed and start cooking as you leave the house the next morning. Make sure you cover the crockpot container well and store in the 'fridge.

Using your crockpot:

- Do not overfill your crockpot. 1/2 to 2/3rds full is optimal. Any fuller than that and you will be steaming your food itself of simmering it.

- If you have prepped your ingredients and filled your crockpot container ahead of time and stored it in the 'fridge, allow the container to come up to room temperature before putting it in the base and turning it on. The dramatic change in temperature from 'fridge to heated base can crack a ceramic container.

- If you're using a traditional crockpot, place a clean dish towel (tea towel) over the top of the crockpot container before putting the lid on. This helps enormously to reduce excess water from building up inside the crockpot and giving you a watery dish. If you are using an Instant Pot on the crockpot setting, make sure that the pressure valve on top of the lid is set to "vent", for the same reason. I do this cloth trick for all recipes, but it is especially important for the crumble recipe, otherwise you run the risk of having a soggy crumble, and no one wants soggy crumble. If you don't want to use a dish towel, you can also use several (and by several I mean like 10) thicknesses of paper towels.

- Place the lid on top of the dish towel or paper towels and lock the lid in place. Again, if you're using an Instant Pot, be sure to check that the pressure valve on the top of the lid is switched to "vent".

- Once cooking has begun – DON'T FIDDLE. Just let it do it's magical cooking thing. Every time you open the lid you are cooling the crockpot and extending the cooking time by 15 – 20 minutes. Some crockpot recipes you can find elsewhere have you taking the lid off to add ingredients at a later time. None of the recipes in this cookbook require that, so just lock that lid on and walk away. Also, curb the urge to stir until it's done!

- Set the crockpot to the appropriate temperature and time. Generally speaking you can vary cooking times to fit your day by using different cooking temperatures, so if the instructions call for 8 hours on low, and you want it faster than that, use the chart below as a guide for using alternate times and temperatures. You can also use the stovetop or oven to cook these recipes, and those times and temperatures are also in the chart.

Note: these recipes are not guaranteed to work in an Instant Pot. If you are familiar with using an Instant Pot you're welcome to give them a try, but for recipes including dairy, and / or alcohol, and also those with little or no liquid added, the recipe will need to be altered in terms of ingredients and method in order to get a great result. Experiment at your own peril!

Crockpot on LOW	Crockpot on HIGH	Oven 350 F / Stovetop
4 – 6 hours	1 ½ - 2 ½ hours	15 – 30 mins
6 – 8 hours	3 – 4 hours	35 – 40 mins
8 – 10 hours	4 – 6 hours	1 ½ - 2 ½ hours

- Please also note that crockpots differ somewhat from each other in their settings, so the above chart is a guide. If you are new to cooking in a crockpot I suggest following the recipe cooking times and temperatures exactly, but if you have been using your crockpot for a while and know it's quirks, adjust time and temp according to your experience of your crockpot. Just know that crockpots (like microwaves) vary, and there is some trial and error involved. Luckily, these recipes are very forgiving, so an extra hour won't destroy dinner. HOORAY!

- Don't forget to turn the crockpot base off once cooking has finished and you have removed the container. You will damage the base if it continues to heat without the container in it.

Post-cooking tweaks:

- Depending on your crockpot, what temperature and time you used to cook the recipe, what cut of meat and the amount of meat you used, and other variables, the amount of water produced during cooking will vary, so don't be alarmed if your sauce / soup is thinner or thicker than you were anticipating or desired. You can easily adjust the sauce's thickness to accommodate such variances as follows.

    o   If your sauce is too thick, simply stir in extra stock or water - 2 fl oz. / ¼ cup at a time - until it is the right thickness for you.

    o   If your sauce is too thin, while stirring with one hand, gently sprinkle ¼ tsp. konjac flour over the surface of the sauce / soup and mix well. Leave for a minute to completely thicken. Repeat in ¼ tsp. increments as required.

Planning ahead with your crockpot

You can make your crockpot even more of an effective and time-efficient meal-making device with these two plan-ahead options:

- Even if there is only 1 or 2 of you in your household, cook the full recipe and freeze whatever you don't eat into 1 or 2 person portions so that you have a standby of ready meals in the freezer that require only defrosting and reheating for dinner to be done.

- Prep the ingredients, place in freezer-strength Ziploc bags or glass containers, label, and freeze uncooked. Remove from the freezer the day before you need them so that they can fully defrost, and then place ingredients into the crockpot on your way out of the door in the morning. Dinner will be done when you walk in the door.

KONJAC FLOUR: WHAT, WHY, HOW

Konjac flour – also known as glucomannan powder – is hands-down the best thickener in a KETO kitchen, and especially when it comes to cooking with a crockpot, konjac is simply magical.

Follow the recipes and only use konjac flour / glucomannan powder as your thickener. DO NOT try and swap it out with guar or xanthan gum (unless you want a sad dinner). There is no other successful KETO sub for konjac. Please avail yourself of some and prepare to be amazed!

Guar and xanthan gums have a different purpose and you will not get the best result if you use them. They have a tendency to become slimy, and do not hold up as well under extremely long cooking times. Guar gum, particularly, loses its thickening abilities in the presence of too much or too long heating. Guar also fails if it is cooked with things that are too acidic or too alkaline.

Here's some good things to know about konjac flour:

- Konjac does not get slimy and is completely tasteless.
- Konjac does not break down or "leak" when heated for a long time.
- Konjac thickens very evenly.
- Konjac is very easy to use, and since it takes a little time to fully thicken it does not clump the instant it is introduced into a liquid.
- Since konjac doesn't clump instantly it is much less stressful and more successful to use than gums. I love it when you're successful in the kitchen!
- When konjac is used in a sauce, gravy or other liquid, it reheats perfectly the next day. It regains the exact same texture and consistency that it had when you first made it, whether you reheat it in the microwave or on the stovetop. Gums, not so much.
- Dishes made with konjac also freeze, defrost and reheat perfectly.
- Konjac is an emulsifier as well as a thickener, so it has the ability to help prevent curdling and separating. This is very good. Curdling is very bad.
- Konjac has about 10x the thickening power of cornstarch (cornflour).
- You use a very small amount of konjac flour, so that pricey tub lasts a very long time.

Here's some tips and tricks when using konjac flour:

- Always use a measuring spoon rather than guessing. Konjac is very strong and you can easily add too much if you don't measure.
- While stirring your sauce or liquids with one hand, gently tap the measuring spoon containing the konjac on the side of the bowl or pan. Alternatively you can sprinkle the konjac evenly over the surface of the liquid and stir rapidly.
- Once you've added the amount in the recipe, if it does not seem thick enough, wait a few minutes to allow the konjac to fully thicken.

More info and where-to-buy konjac here: www.carriebrown.com/archives/23109

COOKING RESOURCES AND Q & A

This cookbook isn't an introduction to a ketogenic or low-carb way of life. It's also not a how-to-cook tome. It's mostly a collection of 40 stupendously tasty ketogenic / low-carb recipes that will make it super-easy for you to get dinner on the table – with the minimum of hands-on time and effort – after a hard day's work.

Almost all of the ingredients you need for these recipes you already have right there in your pantry, or can easily find at the grocery store. This cookbook wasn't intended to be gourmet, or to introduce you to a whole host of new ingredients and techniques. It was intended to give you an array of easy, delicious low-carb and ketogenic dishes that you could toss together to get dinner on the table with the minimum of fuss and effort, in an uncomplicated style that allows you to easily find fresh new recipes to delight your taste buds with.

However, I also get that some of you are new to this way of eating and all that involves. You might also be new to cooking if you've always relied on traditional *fast food* from the freezer section, deli, or drive-through. There might be a few new-to-you ingredients or pieces of equipment. Instead of including all that information in this cookbook I'm including links to the information on my website, so if you need it you can easily grab it, and if you don't need it then you won't have to rifle through that info to get to the recipes.

If you do find you still have questions about ingredients, equipment, or recipes – after checking out the online info at the links included here – there's a Q&A page for this cookbook on my website. Head there and see if the answer is already waiting for you. Feel free to add new questions in the comments and I will update the page with answers as they come in.

Now, let's get cooking!

INFORMATION ON INGREDIENTS
www.carriebrown.com/archives/23109

INFORMATION ON EQUIPMENT
www.carriebrown.com/archives/23310

THE KETO CROCKPOT COOKBOOK Q&A
www.carriebrown.com/eat-smarter-holidays-cookbook-qa

Sage & Bacon Pork with Bacon Cream Sauce

Prep: 10 mins | Cook: 6 hrs + 5 mins | Total: 6 hrs + 15 mins | Serves: 8 - 12

4 TBSP coconut or avocado oil

4 TBSP dried sage

Sea salt and ground black pepper

3 lb. / 1350g pork butt or shoulder

1 lb. / 450g thick-cut bacon slices

¼ cup / 2 fl oz. heavy cream (double cream) *[For dairy-free sub with thick coconut milk]*

½ tsp. konjac flour / glucomannan powder

Mix the oil, dried sage, sea salt and ground black pepper in a small bowl, and using your hands, rub the herbed oil all over the top of the pork.

Lay the slices of bacon over the top of the pork, overlapping each with the one before.

Place the bacon-wrapped pork into the crockpot container, put the lid on, and cook for 6 hours on low. No, you don't need any liquid. Resist the urge to add any!

Carefully lift the cooked pork onto a baking sheet or roasting pan, and brown in the oven under a hot broiler (grill) for 3 – 5 minutes until the bacon is your kind of crispy. Being British my kind of crispy bacon isn't very crispy. You do you.

While the bacon is crisping in the oven, add the cream to juices in the crockpot and blend with an immersion blender until completely smooth. With the other hand, sprinkle the konjac flour over the surface of the sauce and blend for another 20 seconds. Add ½ tsp. more konjac if necessary.

If you don't have an immersion blender, you can also carefully pour all the cooking juices and cream into a blender and blend. Then tap the konjac flour gently through the hole in the blender lid and blend for another 20 seconds. Add ½ tsp. more konjac if necessary.

Remove the pork from the oven and place on a serving dish to rest for 10 minutes. Pour the cream sauce into a jug and serve with the sliced, bacon-wrapped meat.

~~~~~~

Here's what one of my neighbors, Duane, said about this dish after I gifted it to his family:

"I requested this dish for my final meal, and the warden loved it too."

"I loved the bacon gravy. I would have brought it to the Nativity instead of Myrrh."

"I need to double the gravy so I'll have enough to use as aftershave. It is diabolically scrumptious. I ate it all in one sitting. In my food coma I dreamt I was licking bacon gravy off my fingers."

"Truly though, my coworkers were completely jealous of the leftovers I brought for lunch."

Yep, he's a character. He also, **really** loved these juicy pork steaks and, Oh! that bacon gravy!

Pork Chops with Herby Leek Sauce

Prep: 10 mins | Cook: 6 hrs | Total time: 6 hrs + 10 mins | Serves: 6

6 bone-in pork chops

6 oz. / 170g leeks, very finely sliced

1 TBSP dried oregano

1 TBSP dried thyme

Sea salt and black pepper

1 TBSP onion powder

½ tsp. konjac flour / glucomannan powder

1 oz. / 30g butter, melted *[For dairy-free sub with coconut oil]*

2 cloves garlic, crushed

12 fl oz. / 1 ½ cups chicken broth or stock

Place the finely sliced leeks in the bottom or the crockpot, and place the pork chops on top.

In a bowl or jug, mix the dried oregano, dried thyme, sea salt and ground black pepper, onion powder and konjac flour together.

Add the melted butter, crushed garlic, and chicken stock to the mixed dried ingredients and whisk well. Pour the sauce over the pork chops, put the lid on the crockpot, set to low and cook for 6 hours.

Carefully remove the chops from the crockpot and place on plates. Ladle or pour the sauce into a jug or pour directly over the chops and serve.

~~~~~~

Top tip: if your sauce is thicker or thinner than you prefer, see instructions on page 6 to tweak.

Top tip: bone-in pork chops will remain moister than boneless pork chops, so I highly recommend using bone-in. Bone-in pork chops also look a lot prettier, so that's a bonus.

Top tip: increase the fat in this dish (if required) by simply adding extra butter to the top of the pork chop once it is on your plate.

I didn't brown the chops prior to cooking. The gorgeous brown finish you see in the picture was how they looked when I took them from the crockpot. If your chops don't brown as much during cooking, you can pop them on a plate and place them under a hot broiler (grill) for a couple minutes to brown and crisp up the fat, while you're pouring the sauce into a jug for serving.

Sausage Hash Pie

Prep: 10 mins | Cook: 7 hrs | Total: 7 hrs + 10 mins | Serves: 6 - 8

coconut or avocado oil spray

1 lb. / 450g ground pork (sausage meat)

6 oz. / 170g celeriac (celery root), peeled and grated

4 oz. / 110g cheddar cheese, grated

12 eggs

4 TBSP dried chives

¼ cup / 2 fl oz. heavy cream (double cream) *[For dairy-free sub with thick coconut milk]*

¼ tsp. sea salt

ground black pepper to taste

Spray your crockpot container base and sides with coconut or avocado oil, and then either use a crockpot liner, or line the base and sides of the crockpot with parchment paper. This will make getting the pie out of the crockpot in one piece super simple. We like simple. And whole pies.

Over high heat, quickly brown the ground pork, breaking the meat up as you go. You are not trying to cook the meat, but simply brown it, so this will not take very long over a high heat.

Spread half the grated celeriac on the bottom of the crockpot, followed by a layer of half the cheese, and a layer of half the ground pork. Repeat the layers of celeriac, cheese, and ground pork.

In a large bowl, whisk the eggs, dried chives, cream, sea salt and ground black pepper well until the eggs are completely broken up.

Pour the egg mixture over the layers of celeriac, cheese and ground pork in the crockpot.

Place a cloth over the crockpot (see page 5), put the lid on, set to low and cook for 7 hours.

~~~~~~

Top tip: swap the Cheddar out for any exciting hard cheese you like, to switch up the flavor.

This is a perfect recipe to do overnight so that you wake up to awesome on your weekend mornings. Prepare the night before and switch the crockpot on. Go to bed. Wake up. Open the crockpot and remove the pie. Pour the coffee. Slice the pie. DONE.

Also, make this, slice, and freeze in individual portions to grab from the freezer as you head out for a meal-on-the-go during the week. Move over, Starbucks sous vide egg bites. BOOM.

Pork and Fennel Hash

Prep: 10 mins | Cook: 6 hours + 10 mins | Total: 6 hours + 20 mins | Serves 8

1 ¼ lb. / 560g fennel, sliced

3 ½ lb. / 1570g pork loin, cut into 1 ½ " pieces

2 pints / 4 cups chicken stock

8 fl oz. / 1 cup heavy cream (double cream) *[For dairy-free sub with thick coconut milk]*

3 tsp. dried rosemary

sea salt and ground black pepper to taste

2 oz. / 55g butter *[For dairy-free omit]*

1 ½ tsp. konjac flour / glucomannan powder

Spread the fennel slices evenly across the bottom of the crockpot.

Sauté the pork over high heat to brown all the sides. You are not trying to cook the pork, just brown quickly. Place the pork pieces on top of the fennel.

To the pan in which you sautéed the pork, add the stock, cream, rosemary, sea salt, ground black pepper, and butter and stir together until the butter has melted. While stirring with one hand, gently sprinkle the konjac flour over the surface of the sauce and mix well.

Pour the sauce over the pork and fennel in the crockpot.

Put the lid on the crockpot, set to low and cook for 6 hours.

~~~~~~

Top Tip: Go gently and slowly when adding the konjac flour otherwise you will end up with a clumpy sauce. Clumpy sauces are never a good thing. Never.

Top tip: if your hash is thicker or thinner than you prefer, see instructions on page 6 to tweak.

I love fennel. I love it raw, I love it cooked. I love the difference between raw and cooked fennel. How the 'bite' of raw fennel becomes a gentle, soothing flavor once it's been simmered. I love how fennel complements pork so well, allowing both flavors to get a say, no one overpowering the over. I love that fennel comes with pretty, frothy, built-in greenery to garnish stuff with. I love how fennel doesn't turn to mush when cooked, but still retains a hint of crunch – without spoiling the softness of the overall dish. GO, fennel!

"The flavor of the pork came through well with the creamy sauce and fennel. Carrie makes the best creamy sauces!" ~ Craig

Sour Cream BBQ Pulled Pork

Prep: 10 mins | Cook: 8 hours | Total: 8 hours + 10 mins | Serves 6 - 8

3 oz. / 85g onion, finely diced

1 large clove garlic, finely chopped

14 oz. / 390 g can of diced or crushed tomatoes (unsweetened)

1 TBSP coconut aminos

¾ TBSP apple cider vinegar

1 ½ oz. / 40 g xylitol or erythritol

¾ TBSP lemon juice

1 tsp. smoked paprika

½ tsp. sea salt

¾ tsp. liquid smoke

1 tsp. konjac flour / glucomannan powder

2 lb. / 900g pork butt or shoulder

4 oz. / ½ cup sour cream *[For dairy-free omit]*

2 oz. 55g butter *[For dairy-free sub with coconut oil]*

Place the onion, garlic, tomatoes, coconut aminos, apple cider vinegar, sweetener, lemon juice, smoked paprika, sea salt, and liquid smoke in the crockpot and stir well. While still stirring, sprinkle the konjac flour over the surface of the sauce and mix well.

Add the pork to the crockpot. Put the lid on, set to low, and cook for 8 hours.

Remove the lid and carefully lift the pork onto a plate.

Using an immersion blender, blend the sauce in the crockpot until it is smooth. Stir in the sour cream and butter and blend briefly. If you don't have an immersion blender you can also careful pour the sauce and juices into a blender to blend, add the sour cream and butter, and then return to the crockpot.

Return the pork to the crockpot and shred the meat in the sauce using two forks. Stir well until the sauce completely coats every last shred of pork.

~~~~~~

Top tip: if your sauce is thicker or thinner than you prefer, see instructions on page 6 to tweak.

Make up a big batch of this and keep on hand for near-instant meals and no end of fun options!

Carnitas Omelet

Prep: 5 mins | Cook: 5 mins | Total: 5 hours + 15 mins | Serves 1

Sour Cream BBQ Pulled Pork (for recipe see page 19)

3 eggs

1 TBSP water

sea salt and ground black pepper

cheddar cheese, grated *[For dairy-free omit]*

sour cream *[For dairy-free omit]*

scallion (spring onion), chopped

If the Sour Cream BBQ Pulled Pork is not fresh out of the crockpot, gently warm it in the microwave or on the stovetop.

Put a frying pan over high heat for a minute and also turn on the broiler (grill). Whisk the eggs, sea salt and pepper well in a small jug.

Pour the egg mixture into the hot pan and cook without stirring for 30 seconds until the outer 1/8 inch of the edge is firm. The middle will still appear to be completely fluid.

Remove pan from the heat and put under the hot broiler (grill) until the top of the omelet is just set (about 45 seconds).

Remove from under the broiler (grill), shake the pan to free the omelet, and place pan back on the stove.

Spoon the Sour Cream BBQ Pulled Pork onto one half of the omelet, then slide the omelet onto a plate (filled side first) and flip the empty side of the omelet over the pork.

Sprinkle omelet with cheddar cheese, spoon sour cream over the top and sprinkle with scallions.

~~~~~~

We don't need no stinkin' tortillas! Whip up an omelet in a couple of minutes instead of using a tortilla. It doesn't have the same texture or flavor, but it's super-fast, super nutritious, a great source of healthy fat, and tastes delicious. Omelets are something you can eat at any time of day or night, and if you keep some pulled pork, chicken, or beef on hand in the fridge you've got a near-instant plate of incredibly KETO yum in front of you in minutes.

Great food doesn't have to be complicated – switch up the basics to give yourself loads of variety in a heartbeat! I served my Carnitas Omelet with a side of sautéed mushrooms. All the delish!

Lemon Pepper Cream Pork Chops

Prep: 5 mins | Cook: 6 hours | Total time: 6 hours + 5 mins

Bone-in pork chops (see note below)

Lemon pepper

4 fl oz. / ½ cup heavy cream (double cream)

½ tsp. konjac flour / glucomannan powder

Place one layer of chops in the bottom of the crockpot and sprinkle lemon pepper liberally over the chops.

Place the second layer of chops on top of the first and sprinkle liberally with lemon pepper.

Put the lid on the crockpot, set to low, and cook for 6 hours.

Remove the lid and carefully lift the pork chops out onto a warm plate or serving dish.

Add the cream to the juices in the crockpot, and then use your immersion blender to blend the cream and pork juices. Once the sauce is very smooth, and while stirring with one hand, gently sprinkle the konjac flour over the surface and mix well.

If you do not have an immersion blender, you can also carefully pour the liquid from the crockpot into a blender and blend. Once blended, tap the konjac flour through the hole in the blender lid and blend for 5 seconds to incorporate.

Pour the sauce over or around the pork chops and serve.

~~~~~~

Top Tip: Go gently and slowly when adding the konjac flour otherwise you will end up with a clumpy sauce. Pork chops and clumpy sauce are never a good combination.

If you thought that you always need to add liquid to a crockpot in order to not end up with dry meat, think again. These pork chops are moist and delicious, with the cream sauce adding extra fat to the proceedings to make up for pork chops being on the leaner end of the spectrum.

One of the reasons that these chops don't dry out is because they're bone-in. Bone-in meat typically retains more moisture than boneless. I highly recommend that you use bone-in chops for this reason. You may well find that if you use boneless chops the resulting meat will be drier.

Simple. Easy. Fast. Delicious. Add a green salad or side of sautéed non-starchy veggies and in 5 minutes you've got an entire plate of fantastic food, which required almost zero effort.

Carnival Sausages

Prep: 10 mins | Cook: 6 hours | Total: 6 hours + 10 mins | Serves 6 - 8

4 oz. / 110g onion, sliced

2 lbs. / 900g sausages (uncooked)

14 oz. / 390g bell peppers – assorted colors

28 oz. / 785g (large can) crushed or chopped tomatoes (unsweetened)

4 cloves garlic, finely chopped or crushed

2 tsp. dried Italian seasoning herbs

1 tsp. dried basil

1 tsp. dried parsley

1 tsp. sea salt

Spread the sliced onions evenly in the bottom of the crockpot.

Chop the sausages in half, or into large chunks, using a sawing action with a serrated knife so that the soft, raw sausages don't get squashed with the pressure from your knife. Place the sausage pieces in one layer on top of the peppers in the crockpot.

Cut the peppers in half from top to bottom and remove any ribs and seeds. Slice the peppers lengthwise into thin strips, and place them evenly over the sausages in the crockpot.

In a bowl, mix the crushed tomatoes, garlic, Italian seasoning, basil, parsley, and sea salt together well.

Pour the tomato mixture over the peppers in the crockpot.

Put the lid on the crockpot, set to low, and cook for 6 hours.

~~~~~~

Top Tip: Use any of your favorite sausages in this recipe, although it will be especially good with pork sausages. Also, if you like a bit of a kick, using spicy sausages will work well here. You can also add ½ tsp. red pepper flakes to up the heat if that's your thang.

One of the fastest, simplest recipes in the book. Dump it all in and run away. Then pop the lid, give it a gentle (the peppers will be delicate) stir, spoon it into bowls and dinner is done!

"My favorite from this batch of Carrie Brown recipes. So much flavor, texture, and goodness with a touch of heat. And they're pretty! I had them on their own the first night and served them over zucchini noodles on the second. Be sure to double the recipe so you have leftovers!" ~ Minta

Cheesy Sausage Hodgepodge

Prep: 10 mins | Cook: 8 hours | Total: 8 hours + 10 mins | Serves 2 - 4

10 oz. / 280g smoked sausage, sliced

3 oz. / 85g onion, chopped

8 oz. / 225g celeriac (celery root), peeled and cut into very small cubes

4 oz. / 110g cheddar cheese, shredded

6 fl oz. / ¾ cup heavy cream (double cream)

10 fl oz. / 1 ¼ cups chicken stock

4 tsp. nutritional yeast

1 tsp. dried thyme

ground black pepper

1 tsp. konjac flour / glucomannan powder

Place the sliced sausage, chopped onion, cubed celeriac, and shredded cheese in the bottom of the crockpot.

In a bowl, stir the cream, stock, nutritional yeast, thyme, and ground black pepper together, and while stirring with one hand, sprinkle the konjac flour over the sauce and mix well.

Pour the sauce over the ingredients in the crockpot and stir until completely combined.

Put the lid on the crockpot, set to low and cook for 8 hours.

~~~~~~

Top Tip: Go gently and slowly when adding the konjac flour otherwise you will end up with a clumpy sauce. We love a sauce that ain't clumpy. I bet you do, too.

Top tip: if your hodgepodge is thicker or thinner than you prefer, see instructions on page 6 to tweak.

I love smoked foods. One of these days I'm going to just get myself a smoker and start smokin' everything that sits still long enough. Until then, I'm content with smoked cheeses, smoked meats, smoked salts, and boy howdy do I especially love me some smoked sausage. Back in the days when potato salad was a thing in my life I would slice up some smoked sausage and toss that in there, too. And that's what I was thinking about when I came up with this entirely comforting, creamy, steaming bowl of smoky yum.

The celeriac and nutritional yeast add a different flavor profile that you'll keep coming back for.

Shredded Balsamic Beef

Prep: 10 mins | Cook: 7 hrs | Total: 7 hrs + 10 mins | Serves: 12 - 14

1 cup / 8 fl oz. beef stock

3 oz. / 85g erythritol

¼ cup / 2 fl oz. balsamic vinegar

1 TBSP coconut aminos

1 TBSP sea salt

3 cloves fresh garlic, crushed

4 – 5 lb. / 1.8 – 2.25kg tri-tip roast or brisket

Place the beef stock, erythritol, balsamic vinegar, coconut aminos, sea salt and crushed garlic in the crock pot and stir well.

Place the tri-tip or brisket into the crockpot, cover, and cook on low for 7 hours.

Remove the meat from the crock pot and place on a cutting board. Using two forks, shred the meat by pulling it apart. If there are some pieces in the middle that don't shred very easily simply slice them finely with a sharp knife.

Pile the meat back into the crockpot and stir with the sauce until all the meat is completely coated.

~~~~~~

Top tip: if your sauce is thicker or thinner than you prefer, see instructions on page 6 to tweak.

This is 1 of 5 "pulled" recipes in this cookbook, and there's a recipe for what to do with the meat for each of the 5 recipes. Here's some more ideas, so keep some "pulled" goodness on hand:

- Use jicama, coconut, or cauliflower tortillas to make tacos, enchiladas, and quesadillas.
- Use as the protein on top of your salad.
- Use it as a pizza topping on your KETO pizza crust.
- Roll in cabbage leaves and bake to make "egg" rolls.
- Top your KETO waffles with it.
- Wrap in Fathead Dough for empanadas.
- Add mayo and heavy cream to turn into a dip.
- Serve over riced cauliflower.
- Stir it into your cauli-mac and cheese.
- Bake into a crust-less quiche.
- Use in a sandwich using KETO bread.

Shredded Balsamic Beef Boats

Prep: 10 mins | Cook: 7 hours | Total time: 7 hours + 10 mins

large Romaine lettuce leaves

Shredded Balsamic Beef (for recipe see page 29)

avocado, peeled, pitted, and cubed

firm tomatoes, chopped

Cheddar cheese, shredded *[For dairy-free omit]*

fresh cilantro (coriander)

sea salt and ground black pepper

Place the lettuce leaves in dishes or on plates. Dishes work better to stop the boats tipping over sideways and spilling the fillings out. If your lettuce leaves are smaller, use two end-to-end to create one large boat.

Spoon the shredded balsamic beef into each boat.

Sprinkle chunks of avocado and tomato over the meat.

Sprinkle with shredded cheese.

Season with fresh cilantro, sea salt, and ground black pepper.

~~~~~~

When I first embarked on this crockpot cookbook I asked for input from you lovely readers. One request that I got over and over was that there was little to no work required after the crockpot had finished doing its magic.

So while this is not even really a recipe, the goal was to give you an extremely easy, fast, and super-tasty meal you could get on the table within 10 minutes. No time or skill required!

Let your imagination run wild with this one! There are 5 "pulled" recipes in this book so you have options to vary up the type of meat and flavor. Then use your favorite taco toppings to build your own customized boats.

Switch up the cheese to provide an interesting flavor profile. Use different fresh herbs.

Serve with the meat hot, serve with the meat cold. Add additional flavor and fat by topping with sour cream or a KETO-friendly dressing.

The options are endless! 10 minute dinners abound if you've got great pulled meats on your side.

Boozy Braised Beef Short Ribs

Prep: 10 mins | Cook: 7 hours + 10 mins | Total: 7 hours + 20 mins | Serves 4

3 lb. / 1350g beef short ribs

Sea salt and ground black pepper

3 cloves garlic, crushed

1 jar unsweetened tomato / marinara sauce

2 TBSP erythritol

2 TBSP coconut aminos

1 cup / 8 fl oz. beef stock

1 cup / 8 fl oz. Marsala cooking wine

½ tsp. konjac flour / glucomannan powder

Place the short ribs in a pan over high heat, and season with sea salt and ground black pepper. Using tongs, quickly sear and brown all sides of the ribs and then carefully place them in your crockpot.

Put the crushed garlic in the pan you used to brown the beef and sauté over medium heat until just starting to brown. Add the tomato / marinara sauce, erythritol, coconut aminos, beef stock, and Marsala to the pan. Stir well and bring just to the boil. Carefully pour the hot sauce into the crockpot with the ribs, cover, and cook on low for 7 hours.

Very carefully lift the ribs out of the crockpot and place on a serving dish and turn the crockpot to high.

While whisking the liquid in the crockpot rapidly with one hand, gently and slowly shake the konjac flour into the liquid with the other hand. Whisk well for 2 minutes as the sauce thickens.

Spoon the sauce over the ribs and serve.

~~~~~~

Top Tip: Go gently and slowly when adding the konjac flour otherwise you will end up with a clumpy sauce. Who likes a clumpy sauce? *No one raised their hand*.

These ribs are meltingly soft, fall-off-the-bone tender. Now, I never met a beef short rib that I didn't like, but this recipe elevated them to the love level in very short order.

Bonus: short ribs are the fattiest cut of beef (Mmmmm! Flavor!) but also one of the cheapest. And budgets are important. Make KETO work for your budget without missing out on flavor.

Beef Pot Roast

Prep: 10 mins | Cook: 8 hours | Total: 8 hours + 10 mins | Serves 8 - 10

10 oz. / 280g leeks, thickly sliced

10 oz. / 280g celeriac (celery root), peeled and cubed

10 oz. / 280g radishes, quartered

3 ½ lbs. boneless beef rib roast or ribeye roast

sea salt and ground black pepper

Place the thickly sliced leeks, chopped celeriac and radishes evenly over the base of the crockpot.

Place the beef roast on top of the leeks and season liberally with sea salt and ground black pepper.

Put the lid on the crockpot, set to low, and cook for 8 hours.

~~~~~~

Chop, drop, lid, and leave. That's how I wanted to write the recipe, because that's really all you need to do.

Is there an easier way to get dinner on your plate? I admit I was curious as to how a large lump of cow would fare if left to languish in a crockpot all day with zero liquid to keep it company. Now I'm here to tell you that it fares very well.

Meltingly tender meat in a sea of lower-starch veggies with a self-made gravy that you can either thicken or leave as a tasty juice.

The trick to a good crockpot beef pot roast is using a fattier cut of meat such as a rib roast or ribeye roast. These cuts also do even better if you cook them low and slow, so while you could cut the cook time in half by putting on high, a pot roast just gets more and more tender the longer it is cooked. Low and slow is the way to go.

If you're a seasoned crockpotter you will already know that long, slow cooking does a number on colors, but if you're new to crockpotting, heads up: your veggies will lose most of their color, but none of their taste or nutrition. Subdued colors is just part of the crockpot landscape.

A crockpot pot roast is perfect for those days when you have zero time and or energy for cooking, but still want to get a tasty meal in your tummy. Chop, drop, lid, and leave. Then 8 hours later dinner is hot and ready for you to just slice and serve.

Sunday roast with just about zero work. LOVE.

BBQ Pulled Beef

Prep: 5 mins | Cook: 8 hours | Total: 8 hours + 5 mins | Serves 12 - 14

½ recipe KETO BBQ Sauce (see recipe page 85)

3 lbs. / 1350g tri-tip roast or brisket

Pour the BBQ Sauce into the crockpot and place the roast into the sauce.

Put the lid on the crockpot, set to low, and cook for 8 hours.

Using two forks, shred the beef in the crockpot. Once the meat is completely shredded, stir the meat into the sauce.

~~~~~~

Top Tip: If you do not have the KETO BBQ Sauce already made, follow the directions for the Sour Cream BBQ Pulled Pork (see page 19), up to the point where you lift the meat out of the crockpot at the end of the cooking time. Once the beef is removed from the crockpot, use an immersion blender to blend the sauce in the crockpot until it is completely smooth. If you don't have an immersion blender you can also careful pour the sauce and juices into a blender to blend, and then return to the crockpot.

Once the sauce is blended well, place the beef back into the crockpot and shred using two forks. Once the meat is completely shredded, stir the meat into the sauce until the meat is completely coated.

Top tip: if your sauce is thicker or thinner than you prefer, see instructions on page 6 to tweak.

To learn about which the fattiest cuts of meat are on a cow so that you can make the best choices for your crockpot and for general KETO living, we recorded a podcast called, "Cows, part 1". You can listen to it here: http://www.ketovangelistkitchen.com/episode-18-cows-pt-1

We called it "Cows, part 1" because there's always more to talk about when it comes to cows. Cows are important. Also, cows are awesome. And delicious. Cows are delicious.

For this recipe I used tri-tip roast instead of brisket:

1. Because tri-tip is fattier than brisket.

2. Because tri-tip was on sale that weekend and was $5 /lb cheaper than brisket. Saving money is also important. Tri-tip and brisket are interchangeable, so pick which one works best for you.

"The BBQ sauce is yummy and mild and lets the rich beefy taste come through." ~ Minta

BBQ Pulled Beef Tacos

Prep: 15 mins | Cook: 8 hours | Total time: 8 hours + 15 mins

2 oz / 55g Cheddar cheese per taco shell required

BBQ Pulled Beef (see recipe on page 37)

Romaine lettuce, shredded

sour cream *[For diary-free omit]*

firm, fresh tomatoes, chopped

fresh dill, finely chopped

To make the cheese taco shells, line a baking sheet with parchment paper, and then place 2 oz. / 55g shredded cheese per taco in an even layer in rounds on the paper. Leave 1" between each round of cheese. The cheese should be spread evenly, not piled.

Bake the cheese rounds at 350F for 5 – 7 minutes until the cheese is completely melted and the edges start to turn brown. I highly recommend using a kitchen timer so that you don't wander off and forget them, returning to a tray of black, crispy cheese. I am pretty sure black, crispy cheese doesn't taste the best. I like my cheese shells very dark, but you don't have to bake them to the color that I did in the picture.

When the cheese is your preferred color, remove the baking sheet from the oven and let cool for just a minute. Meanwhile, place two glasses (or similar) upside down about 8" part and balance a rolling pin or utensil with a round handle between the two glasses, so it looks like a gym bar.

Use a spatula to carefully lift the cheese round off the baking tray and then drape it in the middle over the rolling pin. Leave the cheese round hanging there until it hardens and then remove. You now have a hard taco shell made entirely of cheese. Repeat for the other cheese rounds. If the cheese shells start to harden on the baking tray before you get to drape them, pop into a warm oven to make them pliable again, and then return to draping operations.

Once you have all your taco shells made, spread a pile of finely shredded Romaine in the bottom of the shells, followed by spoonsful of the BBQ Pulled Beef, and top with sour cream and chopped tomatoes. Finish with fresh chopped dill.

~~~~~~

Top Tip: to easily make finely shredded Romaine, take your whole lettuce and turn it sideways on your cutting board. Starting at the tip of the lettuce, slice cross-wise at 1/4" or 1/8" intervals, depending on how fine you want your shred. Keep cutting until you are 2" from the root.

The Lettuce Episode on our podcast: http://www.ketovangelistkitchen.com/episode-20-lettuce

We Don't Need No Beans Chili

Prep: 5 mins | Cook: 6 hours + 10 mins | Total: 6 hours + 15 mins | Serves 6 - 8

2 lbs. / 900g ground beef (minced beef)

7 oz. / 200g onions, chopped

6 cloves garlic, finely chopped or crushed

1 lb. 12 oz. / 785g can crushed or chopped tomatoes (unsweetened)

1 tsp. sea salt

2 tsp. dried oregano

½ tsp. cayenne

1 tsp. cumin powder

1 ½ tsp. coriander

4 tsp. cocoa powder (unsweetened)

8 fl oz. / 1 cup beef stock

1 ½ tsp. konjac flour / glucomannan powder

Sauté the beef over high heat, breaking the meat up as it browns. The goal is simply to brown it, not cook it. Transfer the browned beef to the crockpot.

Sauté the onions and garlic over high heat, stirring constantly until they caramelize. Over a high heat this will take just a few minutes.

Add the onions, garlic, tomatoes, sea salt, oregano, cayenne, cumin, coriander, cocoa powder and stock to the beef in the crockpot and stir well.

Sprinkle the konjac flour over the surface of the meat and stir well.

Put the lid on the crockpot, set to low and cook for 6 hours.

Serve with shredded Cheddar, sour cream, and scallions (spring onions).

~~~~~~

Top Tip: Go gently and slowly when adding the konjac flour otherwise you will end up with a clumpy sauce. You won't notice clumps in this sauce, but still you don't want them there.

Top tip: if your chili is thicker or thinner than you prefer, see instructions on page 6 to tweak.

"I didn't know chili was worth missing until I took my first bite." ~ Alisen

Beefcake Stew

Prep: 5 mins | Cook: 8 hours + 10 mins | Total: 8 hours + 10 mins | Serves 4 - 6

2 lbs. / 900g tri-tip roast (or similar cut of beef), cut into large chunks

8 fl oz. / 1 cup Bourbon

3 oz. / 85g onion, chopped

2 cloves garlic, finely chopped or crushed

sea salt and ground black pepper

2 tsp. dried thyme

8 fl oz. / 1 cup beef stock

1 ½ tsp konjac flour / glucomannan powder

12 oz. / 340g mushroom variety – cremini / shitake / oyster / button, chopped

Sauté the beef chunks over high heat to brown them on all sides. You are not trying to cook the meat, just brown the outside. Fast and furious over high heat will do this.

Transfer the meat to the crockpot.

Deglaze the pan by carefully adding the Bourbon and stirring well.

Add the onion, garlic, sea salt and ground black pepper, thyme, and beef stock and stir well.

While stirring with one hand gently sprinkle the konjac flour over the surface and mix well.

Add the mushrooms to the pan, stir well, and then pour the mushrooms and sauce into the crockpot over the meat.

Put the lid on the crockpot, set to low and cook for 8 hours.

~~~~~~

Top Tip: Go gently and slowly when adding the konjac flour otherwise you will end up with a clumpy sauce. I can't think of one instance when a clumpy sauce is a good thing. Not one.

Top tip: if your stew is thicker or thinner than you prefer, see instructions on page 6 to tweak.

This beef stew is for Danny Vega and his gorgeous wife, Maura. Danny does amazing work over on The Ketogenic Athlete website and podcast, so when he asked for a crockpot beef stew I was thrilled to oblige. If you've ever seen Danny, you'll know why I had to call it Beefcake Stew ☺

"The best beef stew I've ever had." ~ Craig

Mighty Meat Pizza

Prep: 10 mins | Cook: 6 hours + 5 mins | Total: 6 hours + 15 mins | Serves 4 - 8

2 lbs. / 900g ground beef (minced beef)

3 oz. / 85g cream cheese

3 oz. / 85g mozzarella cheese, shredded

Coconut or avocado oil spray

14 oz. / 390g (small can) crushed tomatoes (unsweetened)

2 cloves garlic, finely chopped or crushed

1 tsp. dried Italian seasoning herbs

½ tsp. dried basil

½ tsp. dried parsley

½ tsp. sea salt

2 oz. / 55g mozzarella cheese, shredded

2 oz. / 55g cheddar cheese, shredded

5 oz. / 110g pepperoni

6 oz. / 110g mushrooms, sliced

Over high heat, break up and brown the ground beef. You don't need to cook it through, just brown the outside. Once the beef is browned, turn the heat off and add the cream cheese, stirring constantly until the cream cheese is completely melted and stirred through. Add the 3 oz. / 85g shredded mozzarella and quickly stir to mix together.

Spray the crockpot with oil and spread the beef and cheese mixture evenly on the bottom..

In a bowl, mix the crushed tomatoes, garlic, Italian seasoning, basil, parsley, and sea salt together well. Pour the tomato mixture over the meat in the crockpot.

Spread the shredded mozzarella and cheddar cheeses evenly over the tomato sauce, and then place the pepperoni and mushroom slices evenly over the top.

Put the lid on the crockpot, set to low, and cook for 6 hours.

~~~~~~

Change it up by using any of your favorite pizza toppings. Also great warmed up for lunch.

"This totally scratched my pizza itch!" ~ *Penny*

Sour Cream Mushroom Short Ribs

Prep: 5 mins | Cook: 8 hours + 15 mins | Total: 8 hours + 20 mins | Serves 6 - 8

4 lbs. / 1.8kg beef short ribs (I used the long flat ones for this recipe)

3 oz. / 85g onions, finely chopped

4 fl oz. / ½ cup red wine

2 oz. / 55g butter

3 tsp. dried parsley

sea salt and ground black pepper to taste

1 lb. / 450g mushrooms, roughly chopped

2 TBSP lemon juice

8 fl oz. / 1 cup sour cream

Sauté the short ribs over a high heat to brown the outsides. You are not trying to cook them, just brown them, so fast and furious will achieve this. Unless you have a ginormous pan you will need to do this in batches. Once brown, place the ribs in the crockpot.

Add the chopped onions to the pan and sauté for a few minutes to brown them. Add the red wine and stir well to deglaze the pan. Add the butter and stir well. Add the parsley, sea salt and ground black pepper.

Put the mushrooms in the crockpot on top of the meat and then pour the sauce over the mushrooms.

Put the lid on the crockpot, set to low and cook for 8 hours.

Remove the lid and carefully lift out the ribs onto a warm dish.

Carefully pour the mushroom sauce into a blender, add the lemon juice and sour cream and blend it on high until it is completely smooth and thick. Mushrooms take more to blend than you might imagine. I doubt your immersion will do the trick, so suggest you go straight for the blender.

Pour the sour cream mushroom sauce over the short ribs and serve.

~~~~~~

"This recipe should come with a warning. I couldn't stop eating it. I found myself going back for seconds and thirds. It is best served to a large crowd or you will want to eat the whole thing yourself. I guarantee your friends will want the recipe." ~ Alisen

Clam Chowder

Prep: 10 mins | Cook: 8 hours | Total: 8 hours + 10 mins | Serves 4 - 6

4 oz. / 110g onion, chopped

4 oz. / 110g celery, chopped

2 cloves garlic, finely chopped or crushed

8 oz. / 225g radishes, cut into small cubes

8 oz. / 225g celeriac (celery root), peeled and cut into small cubes

20 oz. / 560g clam meat (this is the amount of meat in the large 3 lb. 3oz. / 1.445 kg can)

6 oz. / 170g bacon, cooked and chopped

1 oz. / 30 g butter

12 fl oz. / 1 ½ cups heavy cream (double cream)

8 fl oz. / 1 cup clam juice (from the can above)

3 tsp. konjac flour / glucomannan powder

1 ½ pints / 3 cups chicken stock

1 TBSP white wine vinegar

½ tsp. dried thyme

Sea salt and ground black pepper

Add the onion, celery, garlic, radishes, celeriac, clam meat, bacon, and butter to the crockpot.

In a bowl add the cream and clam juice, and while stirring with one hand sprinkle the konjac flour gently over the surface of the liquid and mix well. Stir in the chicken stock, white wine vinegar, thyme, sea salt, and ground black pepper. Pour the sauce over the clams and veggies in the crockpot and mix until combined.

Put the lid on the crockpot, set to low and cook for 8 hours.

~~~~~~

Top Tip: Go gently and slowly when adding the konjac flour otherwise you will end up with a clumpy sauce. Un-clumpy sauce is good. Really good.

Top tip: if your chowder is thicker or thinner than you prefer, see instructions on page 6 to tweak.

"Yummy! My 'Clam Chowder Expert' husband loved it, and to this day does not know he was not eating potatoes!" ~ Minta

Hammered Chicken

Prep: 5 mins | Cook: 4 hrs | Total time: 4 hrs + 5 mins | Serves: 6 - 8

½ tsp. ginger, crushed

2 cloves fresh garlic, crushed

½ cup / 4 fl oz. chicken stock

2 oz. / 55g erythritol

2 TBSP tomato paste

3 TBSP apple cider vinegar

¼ cup / 2 fl oz. Bourbon

¼ cup / 2 fl oz. coconut aminos

3 lbs. / 1.35kg boneless, skinless chicken thighs, cut into 1" pieces

½ tsp. konjac flour / glucomannan powder (if required)

Place the crushed ginger, crushed garlic, stock, erythritol, tomato paste, apple cider vinegar, Bourbon, and coconut aminos in the crock pot and stir until completely mixed.

Add the chopped chicken and stir to coat the pieces evenly. Cook on low for 4 hours.

If you like a thicker sauce, slowly and gently tap the konjac flour into the chicken sauce while stirring rapidly with the other hand. Cook for a minute or two until the sauce has thickened, and serve.

~~~~~~

One of the questions many people have when they embark on a KETO / Low-carb lifestyle is whether or not they can consume alcohol. So because we're here to help, and here to make your KETO journey clearer and easier, we recorded a podcast for you all about cooking with alcohol.

You can listen to it here: http://www.ketovangelistkitchen.com/episode-11-cooking-with-alcohol

Spoiler Alert: if you look at the ingredients in this recipe you'll see some Bourbon. So yes, you can cook with alcohol, but there's caveats. I know, there's always caveats, huh? Listen in and get the full scoop.

In cooking, the alcohol is there for flavor, not to make you fall over, but if alcohol is something you'd rather avoid altogether then feel free to swap out the booze for extra stock. The flavor will be different, but it'll still taste good. It's important that you do you when it comes to alcohol.

Bacon Tarragon Smothered Chicken

Prep: 5 mins | Cook: 4 hours + 15 mins | Total: 4 hours + 20 mins | Serves: 4 - 6

6 oz. / 170g onion, finely chopped

6 oz. / 170g green pepper, finely chopped

1 TBSP dried tarragon

½ cup / 4 fl oz. chicken stock

2 lbs. / 900g bone-in chicken thighs, skin-on

12 oz. / 340g bacon

8 oz. / 225g cream cheese

½ tsp. konjac flour / glucomannan powder (if required)

Sea salt and ground black pepper

Put the chopped onions and peppers in the crockpot, sprinkle the dried tarragon over the top, pour in the chicken stock and stir.

Place the chicken thighs on top of the vegetables and stock, and cook for 4 hours on low.

At the end of the cooking time, cook the bacon in the oven for 15 minutes at 400F. While the bacon is cooking, carefully lift the chicken thighs out of the crockpot and into a serving dish.

Add the cream cheese to the juices in the crock pot, turn the crock pot to high and stir until the cream cheese has melted.

If you want the sauce to be thicker, slowly tap the konjac flour into the sauce while whisking well with the other hand.

When the bacon is cooked, carefully remove it from the baking sheet and, using scissors, cut it into pieces and add to the sauce, stirring well.

Season with sea salt and ground black pepper to taste and pour the bacon tarragon sauce over the chicken and serve.

~~~~~~

This is my favorite recipe from the whole cookbook. OK, well, maybe the Strawberry Surprise Crumble and the Nicer Than Rice Pudding would vie for that slot, but in the dinner department this Bacon Tarragon Smothered Chicken rocked my world. I could eat this every might for a really long time and love every minute of it. If you have never tried tarragon I urge you to make this the next thing you crock from this cookbook!

Sweet and Sour Shredded Chicken

Prep: 10 mins | Cook: 8 hours | Total: 8 hours + 10 mins | Serves 8 - 10

4 fl oz. / ½ cup ketchup (unsweetened)

6 fl oz. / ¾ cup apple cider vinegar

4 oz. / 110g erythritol

2 TBSP coconut aminos

1 ½ TBSP dried mustard powder

sea salt and black pepper to taste

1 tsp. konjac flour / glucomannan powder

3 lbs. / 1350g skinless chicken thighs, legs, or wings (bone-in or boneless)

Put the ketchup, apple cider vinegar, erythritol, coconut aminos, mustard powder, and sea salt and pepper in the bottom of the crockpot and stir well.

While stirring with one hand, sprinkle the konjac flour gently over the surface of the sauce and mix well. Add the chicken to the crockpot and toss in the sauce. Put the lid on the crockpot, set to low and cook for 8 hours.

Remove the lid and shred the chicken using two forks. If you used bone-in chicken be very careful to remove all the bones as you shred the meat.

Mix with the sauce until shredded chicken is completely coated.

~~~~~~

Top Tip: Go gently and slowly when adding the konjac flour otherwise you will end up with a clumpy sauce. There is no room for clumpy sauce in your life.

Top tip: if your sauce is thicker or thinner than you prefer, see instructions on page 6 to tweak.

When I posted this picture on Facebook with the caption "Sweet and Sour Shredded Chicken", everyone went nuts. Seems sweet and sour is a very popular thing around these parts. A lot of folks miss the whole glorious Asian flavor when going low-carb or KETO. This recipe = happy.

It can be used in a multitude of ways (see page 29 for a list of ideas) so if you love sweet and sour I am a big advocate of keeping some of this in your freezer at all times so you can whip up some Asian-flavored awesomeness whenever the mood takes you.

There's one simple idea for turning Sweet and Sour Shredded Chicken into dinner over the page.

Sweet and Sour Shredded Chicken Cucumber Lettuce Wraps

Prep: 10 mins | Cook: 8 hours + 10 mins | Total: 8 hours + 10 mins

Butter lettuce

Sweet and Sour Shredded Chicken (recipe on page 55)

cucumber, julienned

sour cream

scallions (spring onions), sliced

sea salt and ground black pepper

Place Butter lettuce leaves on plates or in dishes.

Spoon Sweet and Sour Shredded Chicken into each lettuce leaf.

Place julienned cucumber on top of the chicken, and then spoon sour cream over the cucumber.

Sprinkle with scallions (spring onions), and season with sea salt and ground black pepper.

~~~~~~

Top tip: the best and easiest way to julienne cucumber is to use a julienne peeler (see resources on page 9). You can also use a mandolin if you have one, or the large side of a box grater. Or, if you are adept with a sharp knife you can slice into fine strips.

I love the contrast of the sweet and sour flavors with the crisp, fresh lettuce and crunchy cucumbers. When I came up with this combination for the lettuce wraps I was remembering eating crispy duck pancakes in London many years ago. You place shredded duck, plum sauce and crisp cucumber into a Chinese pancake, roll them up and eat them. It was one of my favorites, and I was especially taken with the contrast between the crisp cucumber, the sweet sauce and the soft duck.

You can go to town with lettuce wraps, making up any number of variations. By making a huge pot of this Sweet and Sour Shredded Chicken and keeping some in portions in the freezer you can have hot and delicious meals ready to go in no time.

There's a list of other ideas for you on page 29.

Butter lettuce is one of my favorite lettuces. As well as being super pretty, and a fabulous bright green color that will brighten up any plate, Butter lettuce is softer and creamier than other varieties and has a gentle, almost sweet flavor. It is often also called Boston lettuce or Bibb lettuce, so keep a lookout for it at the grocery store if it's a new-to-you variety. It is often sold in a plastic container with its root still on – a living lettuce, if you will.

Fiesta Chicken Spaghetti

Prep: 10 mins | Cook: 6 hours | Total: 6 hours + 10 mins | Serves 6 - 8

1 lb. / 450g bell peppers, assorted colors

3 lbs. / 1350g boneless, skinless chicken, cut into 1" pieces

4 cloves garlic, finely chopped or crushed

14 oz. / 390g can of crushed or chopped tomatoes (unsweetened)

2 tsp. dried basil

2 tsp. onion powder

sea salt and ground black pepper to taste

1 pint / 2 cups chicken stock

3 ½ tsp. konjac flour / glucomannan powder

1 oz. / 30g butter

2 x 8 oz. / 225g packets shirataki spaghetti, washed, rinsed and drained well

parmesan cheese, grated, to garnish

Cut the peppers in half lengthwise and remove the ribs and seeds, then slice into strips lengthwise. Cut the strips in half to make shorter strips. Place in bottom of crockpot.

Place the chicken pieces on top of the peppers.

In a bowl add the garlic, tomatoes, basil, onion powder, sea salt and pepper, and stock, and stir together. While stirring with one hand, gently sprinkle the konjac flour over the surface and mix well.

Pour the sauce over the chicken and peppers, put the lid on the crockpot, set to low and cook for 6 hours.

Remove the lid and stir in the rinsed, drained shirataki spaghetti. Spoon into bowls and sprinkle with grated parmesan cheese.

~~~~~~

Top Tip: Go gently and slowly when adding the konjac flour otherwise you will end up with a clumpy sauce. Clump-free sauce for the win!

Top tip: if your sauce is thicker or thinner than you prefer, see instructions on page 6 to tweak.

Top tip: cut the shirataki spaghetti in half to make it easier to stir into the chicken sauce.

Creamy Basil Chicken Marsala

Prep time: 5 mins | Cook time: 5 hours + 10 mins | Total time: 5 hours + 15 mins | Serves 4

8 skin-on, bone-in chicken thighs

Sea salt and ground black pepper

5 oz. / 140g wild mushrooms (whatever kind of wild you fancy), chopped

¾ cup / 6 fl oz. Marsala cooking wine

¼ cup / 2 fl oz. chicken stock

½ cup / 8 fl oz. heavy cream (double cream) *[For dairy-free sub with thick coconut milk]*

2 tsp. erythritol

1 tsp. sea salt

1 ½ tsp. konjac flour / glucomannan powder

8 large fresh basil leaves, shredded

Sprinkle sea salt and black pepper on the skin of the chicken thighs and then put them **skin side down** in a pan over high heat. You're not trying to cook the chicken, you're only crisping and browning that gorgeous skin, so fast and furious in the frying pan is what we need. You do not need to turn and cook the other side. This will only take a few minutes.

Once the skin is golden and crisp, use tongs and carefully place the chicken pieces **skin side up** in a single layer in your crockpot. Scatter the chopped mushrooms over the chicken and then pour the Marsala and chicken stock over the top. Cover and cook on low for 5 hours.

Carefully remove the chicken pieces from the crockpot and place in a serving dish, skin side up, and then turn the crockpot to high and add the cream.

Into a small dish measure the erythritol, sea salt, and konjac flour and mix well.

While whisking the liquid in the crockpot rapidly with one hand, gently and slowly shake the konjac flour mixture into the liquid with the other hand. Whisk well for 2 minutes as the sauce thickens. Once the sauce has thickened, stir in the fresh basil and pour the sauce over the chicken.

~~~~~~

Top Tip: Go gently and slowly when adding the konjac flour mixture otherwise you will end up with a clumpy sauce. I can't think of one instance when a clumpy sauce is a good thing. Not one.

Your '15-minutes-of-effort-but-completely-wow-the-pants-off-your-guests' entree. You're welcome.

Crunchy Cashew Chicken

Prep: 5 mins | Cook: 4 hours + 10 mins | Total: 4 hours + 15 mins | Serves 6 - 8

1 TBSP coconut or avocado oil

2 lbs. / 900g boneless, skinless chicken pieces, cut into 1" pieces

3 TBSP tomato paste (unsweetened)

3 TBSP white wine vinegar

4 ½ TBSP coconut aminos

2 TBSP erythritol

3 cloves garlic, minced

1 tsp. fresh ginger, minced

sea salt and ground black pepper

½ tsp. konjac flour / glucomannan powder (if required)

3 oz. / 85g cashews, roughly chopped

Heat the oil in a pan on high, add the chicken pieces, and quickly brown on all sides. You are not trying to cook the chicken, just brown it. Fast and furious over high heat will do the trick.

To the crockpot add the tomato paste, white wine vinegar, coconut aminos, erythritol, minced garlic, minced ginger, sea salt and ground black pepper, and whisk together to make a sauce.

Add the chicken pieces to the crockpot and toss in the sauce until they are evenly coated.

Put the lid on the crockpot, set to low, and cook for 4 hours.

If you want the sauce to be thicker (the amount of water chicken releases during slow cooking varies), slowly tap the konjac flour into the chicken sauce while stirring well with the other hand.

Add the roughly chopped cashews, stir, and spoon into bowls over cauli-rice.

~~~~~~

Top Tip: Go gently and slowly when adding the konjac flour mixture otherwise you will end up with a clumpy sauce. Smooth sauce all the way, baby!

Nuts can be quite a large part of a KETO / Low-carb lifestyle, so we recorded you a podcast all about nuts. Even if you know everything there is to know about nuts, you should listen, because if nothing else it will give you a giggle. Laugh and learn. Or just laugh. Because laughing is good.

http://www.ketovangelistkitchen.com/episode-8-nuts

BBQ Pull-apart Chicken

Prep: 5 mins | Cook: 8 hours | Total: 8 hours + 5 mins | Serves 8 - 10

½ recipe KETO BBQ Sauce (see recipe page 85)

3 lbs. / 900g skinless chicken thighs, legs, or wings (bone-in or boneless)

Pour the BBQ Sauce into the crockpot and place the chicken pieces into the sauce.

Put the lid on the crockpot, set to low, and cook for 8 hours.

Using two forks, shred the chicken. If you used bone-in chicken be very careful to remove all the bones as you shred the meat.

Once the meat is completely shredded, stir the meat into the sauce.

~~~~~~

Top Tip: If you do not have the KETO BBQ Sauce already made, follow the directions for the Sour Cream BBQ Pulled Pork (see page 19), up to the point where you lift the meat out of the crockpot at the end of the cooking time. Once the chicken is removed from the crockpot, use an immersion blender to blend the sauce in the crockpot until it is completely smooth. If you don't have an immersion blender you can also careful pour the sauce and juices into a blender to blend, and then return to the crockpot.

Once the sauce is blended well, place the chicken back into the crockpot and shred using two forks. Once the meat is completely shredded, stir the meat into the sauce.

Top tip: if your sauce is thicker or thinner than you prefer, see instructions on page 6 to tweak.

Shredded or Pulled meats can be the hero of a KETO kitchen. I've given you 5 different ways to use it in this book, and on page 29 you'll find a list of other ideas for using the meat.

Carnitas Omelet – page 21

BBQ Pulled Beef Tacos – page 39

Shredded Balsamic Beef Boats – page 31

Double Cheese BBQ Chicken Melts – page 67

Sweet and our Pulled Chicken Cucumber Lettuce Wraps – page 57

"Carrie's BBQ Sauce does it again – a mild tangy flavor that really compliments the meat of choice. The chicken was tender and moist. I served mine on shredded cabbage." ~ Minta

Double Cheese BBQ Chicken Melts

Prep: 10 mins | Cook: 8 hrs + 5 mins | Total: 8 hrs + 15 mins | Serves: 4

coconut or avocado oil spray

8 large Portobello mushrooms

12 oz. / 335g ricotta cheese

Sea salt and ground black pepper to taste

3 TBSP fresh thyme, finely chopped

½ recipe BBQ Pull-apart Chicken (see page 65)

3 – 6 oz. / 85 – 170 g mozzarella, grated

Spray a baking sheet with coconut or avocado oil spray. Place the mushrooms upside down on the tray and broil (grill) for about 6 minutes until tender.

While the mushrooms are broiling (grilling), season the ricotta with sea salt and ground black pepper and add the finely chopped fresh thyme. Stir to combine.

Remove mushrooms from under the broiler (grill), leaving them on the baking sheet.

Spread the herbed ricotta evenly over the mushrooms and then pile BBQ Pull-apart Chicken on top of the ricotta.

Sprinkle grated mozzarella evenly over the stuffed mushrooms and place under the broiler (grill) for a few minutes until the cheese is melted and golden.

Use a spatula to carefully lift each mushroom onto a plate.

~~~~~~

These babies made me entirely happy. I've always been a huge mushroom fan, but adding two different types of cheese, meltingly soft chicken, BBQ sauce, and some fresh thyme only served to make them even better.

There's more ideas for using BBQ Pull-apart Chicken on page 29. This is a recipe you should make in big batches and keep in the freezer for those times when you need a tasty dinner in short order. It's pretty much a kitchen staple like mayonnaise and ketchup you can do so many things with it!

If after eating this you love the whole portabella mushroom *thang*, hop on up to The Ketovangelist Kitchen to make yourself some completely delicious Mushroom Tuna Melts:
http://www.ketovangelistkitchen.com/mushroom-tuna-melt

Mushroom Cream Chicken Stroganoff

Prep: 5 mins | Cook: 6 hours, 5 mins | Total: 6 hours 10 mins | Serves 4 - 6

2 lbs. / 900g skinless, boneless chicken, cut into 1" pieces

8 oz. / 225g cream cheese

2 fl oz. / ¼ cup heavy cream (double cream) *[For dairy-free sub with thick coconut milk]*

4 fl oz. / ½ cup chicken stock

3 tsp. onion powder

½ tsp. sea salt

ground black pepper to taste

2 TBSP white wine vinegar

8 oz. / 225g mushrooms, sliced

½ tsp. konjac flour / glucomannan powder

1 x 8 oz. / 225g packet shirataki fettucine, washed, rinsed, and drained well

Place the chicken pieces in the bottom of the crockpot.

To a pan, add the cream cheese, cream, and chicken stock, and stir well over medium heat until the cream cheese is melted. Add the onion powder, sea salt and ground black pepper, white wine vinegar, and mushrooms, and mix well.

While stirring rapidly with one hand, sprinkle the konjac flour gently over the surface of the sauce and mix well. Pour the sauce over the chicken pieces in the crockpot and stir.

Put the lid on the crockpot, set to low and cook for 6 hours.

Remove the lid and stir in the rinsed, drained shirataki fettucine. Note: you can cut the fettucine in half with scissors to make it easier to stir into the chicken and mushroom sauce.

~~~~~~

Top Tip: Go gently and slowly when adding the konjac flour otherwise you will end up with a clumpy sauce. You don't want a clumpy sauce. No sirree.

Top tip: if your stroganoff is thicker or thinner than you prefer, see instructions on page 6 to tweak.

"Having a crockpot full of KETO Stroganoff ready to eat when you walk in the door is the best thing you could do for yourself after a hard day at work. It was entirely good for the body and the soul." ~ Duane

Tangy Thyme Chicken Meatballs

Prep: 15 mins | Cook: 4 hours + 10 mins | Total: 4 hours + 25 mins | Serves 4 - 6

1 ½ oz. / 40g. pork rinds

1 ½ lbs. / 670g ground chicken (minced chicken)

2 tsp. dried thyme

2 eggs

1 ½ oz. / 40g coconut flour

14 oz. / 390g (small can) canned crushed tomatoes (unsweetened)

3 TBSP coconut aminos

3 TBSP white wine vinegar

3 TBSP erythritol

1 tsp. garlic powder

1 tsp. onion powder

½ tsp. konjac flour / glucomannan powder

Puff the pork rinds in the microwave for 3 minutes on high (note: microwaves vary so this is a guide) or in the oven at 450F for 5 minutes. Let cool. Grind in a food processor or coffee grinder.

Pour ground rinds into a bowl and add the minced chicken, dried thyme, eggs, and coconut flour to mix well until completely combined. Using your hands, roll the meat mixture into 1" balls and place on an oiled baking sheet. Place meatballs in the oven and bake for 10 minutes at 350 F.

While the meatballs are baking, add the tomatoes, coconut aminos, white wine vinegar, erythritol, garlic powder, and onion powder to a bowl and mix well. While stirring with one hand, gently sprinkle the konjac flour over the surface and mix well.

Remove the meatballs from the oven, and using a spoon, transfer them to the crockpot. Pour the sauce over the meatballs and stir to coat.

Put the lid on the crockpot, set to low, and cook for 4 hours.

~~~~~~

Top Tip: Go gently and slowly when adding the konjac flour otherwise you will end up with a clumpy sauce. Clumpy free = awesome. Everyone wants clump-free sauce.

Top tip: if your sauce is thicker or thinner than you prefer, see instructions on page 6 to tweak.

Serve over your favorite non-starchy *thing* – cauliflower, broccoli, shirataki, zucchini noodles.

Bacon, Leek and Chicken Ragout

Prep: 5 mins | Cook: 6 hours + 10 mins | Total: 6 hours + 15 mins | Serves 4 - 6

12 oz. / 340g bacon, chopped

1lb 4oz. / 560g leeks, sliced

2 lbs. / 900g boneless, skinless chicken breasts, cut into 1" pieces

8 fl oz. / 1 cup heavy cream (double cream) *[For dairy-free sub with thick coconut milk]*

1 ½ pints / 3 cups chicken stock

4 tsp. oregano

4 tsp. onion powder

1 tsp. apple cider vinegar

2 tsp. konjac flour / glucomannan powder

Sauté the chopped bacon until it is browned.

Meanwhile, place the sliced leeks in the bottom of the crockpot, and place the chicken pieces on top of the leeks, followed by the cooked bacon pieces.

To the bacon grease in the pan add the cream, stock, oregano, onion powder, apple cider vinegar, and stir well. While stirring with one hand gently sprinkle the konjac flour over the surface of the sauce and mix well.

Pour the sauce over the ingredients in the crockpot.

Put the lid on the crockpot, set to low and cook for 6 hours.

~~~~~~

Top Tip: Go gently and slowly when adding the konjac flour otherwise you will end up with a clumpy sauce. Silky smooth sauce is the only way to go!

Top tip: if your ragout is thicker or thinner than you prefer, see instructions on page 6 to tweak.

This. This! This is like all my favorite things crockpotted into a warm, creamy, bowlful of awesome.

This would be perfect frozen into portions so you can grab-and-go for a hot lunch at the office – just gently microwave to re-heat and ward off the envious gazes of your workmates as they smell the delicious wafting from your dish.

We recorded a podcast all about leeks! http://www.ketovangelistkitchen.com/episode-27-leeks/

Whole Rosemary Lemon Chicken

Prep: 5 mins | Cook: varies – see chart | Total: varies – see chart | Serves 4 - 8

1 whole chicken

4 whole lemons

8 – 10 springs of fresh rosemary

8 oz. / 225g onions, chopped into thick chunks or slices

Remove all the packaging and the giblets (the bag of bits inside, if there is one) from your chicken.

Cut 3 of the lemons into 8 wedges each and push them into the cavity of the chicken, along with 3 – 4 sprigs of rosemary. If you have a small chicken put the other lemon wedges in the crockpot. Slice the remaining lemon into thin slices.

Chop the onions into thick slices and spread over the bottom of the crockpot.

Place the lemon and rosemary stuffed chicken on top of the bed of onions.

Lay the lemon slices and remaining sprigs of rosemary on the chicken – tucking them between the body and the legs and wings, and laying them on top.

Cover and cook per this chart:

2 - 2.5 lbs. → 6 - 8 hours on low or 3-4 hours on high

3 - 4 lbs. → 7 - 9 hours on low or 3.5 - 4.5 hours on high

4.5 - 5 lbs. → 8 - 10 hours on low or 4-5 hours on high

Remove the lid, and if you have a removable oven-safe liner in your crockpot, carefully lift it from the crockpot base and put it under a pre-heated broiler (grill) and brown the chicken skin. Don't walk away! This only takes about 3 minutes and you don't want burnt chicken!

If your crockpot does not have a removable oven-safe liner, then carefully lift your chicken out of the crockpot and onto a baking sheet before placing under the broiler (grill).

~~~~~~

This might just be the juiciest, loveliest "roast" chicken you've ever had. And I have a suspicion that I won't be roasting chickens any more. I'll be crockpotting them. And then crockpotting the carcass into the most fantastic chicken stock ever. How? That's right on the next page.

Chicken Bone Broth

Prep: 5 mins | Cook: 8 - 10 hours | Total: 8 - 10 hours + 5 mins

Whole chicken carcass + bones from legs and wings

Onions, finely chopped

Celery, finely chopped

Selection of dried herbs

Water

Place your chicken carcass and bones in the crockpot.

Add 2 – 3 cups of chopped veggies that you have on hand, 3 – 4 tsp. of your favorite dried herbs, and 2 – 3 pints / 4 – 6 cups water.

Put the lid on the crockpot, set to low and simmer for 10 hours.

Remove the lid from the crockpot, and leave to cool until it's no longer steaming.

Carefully lift out all the bones and discard.

Place a sieve over a large bowl and carefully pour the bone broth through the sieve to catch all the veggies and any remaining small bones.

Pass the bone broth through a finer sieve to remove more of the solids if you want a completely clear stock.

Pour into a glass storage jar and keep in the 'fridge, or freeze in the freezer.

~~~~~~

If you've never had homemade stock or broth then now's the time to discover the difference. In the spirit of full disclosure, I almost never make my own stock, but that's mostly because I am single and it takes me 6 months to save up enough bones to make a pot. Before the chicken that I crockpotted for this cookbook, I cannot remember the last time I roasted a whole chicken. While I love everything about cooking for other people – be it for cookbooks or the blog or for real live in-person people – cooking for myself is another matter. It just never crosses my mind to cook a whole chicken, although I have to say, now I've done one in a crockpot it's definitely on my radar as the way to get myself a big ole pile of delicious chicken meat to use in other dishes.

The nutritional benefits of bone broth are extensive – way too much to even begin to cover here, so I urge you to get on the Interwebs and do research. Then grab yourself a chicken and crockpot your way to some bone brothy health. It also tastes better than store bought. Just sayin'.

Wild Chicken and Rice Soup

Prep: 5 mins | Cook: 6 hours, 5 mins | Total: 6 hours 10 mins | Serves 4 - 8

2 lbs. / 900g skinless, boneless chicken, cut into 1" pieces

8 oz. / 225g cream cheese

8 fl oz. / 1 cup heavy cream (double cream)

8 fl oz. / 1 cup chicken stock

2 tsp. garlic powder

4 tsp. dried thyme

2 TBSP lemon juice

1 tsp. sea salt

ground black pepper

4 oz. / 110g onion, chopped

4 oz. / 110g celery, chopped

1 ½ tsp. konjac flour / glucomannan powder

2 x 8 oz. / 225g packets shirataki rice, rinsed well in cold water and drained well

2 pints / 4 cups chicken stock

Place the chicken pieces in the bottom of the crockpot.

To a pan, add the cream cheese, cream, and 8 fl oz. / 1 cup chicken stock, and stir well over medium heat until the cream cheese is melted. Add the garlic powder, thyme, lemon juice, sea salt and ground black pepper, onion, and celery and mix well.

While stirring rapidly with one hand, sprinkle the konjac flour gently over the surface of the sauce and mix well. Pour the sauce over the chicken pieces in the crockpot and stir.

Put the lid on the crockpot, set to low and cook for 6 hours.

Remove lid and stir in the rinsed, drained shirataki rice and final 2 pints / 4 cups chicken stock.

~~~~~~

Top Tip: Go gently and slowly when adding the konjac flour otherwise you will end up with a clumpy sauce. Down with clumpy sauces!

Top tip: if your soup is thicker or thinner than you prefer, see instructions on page 6 to tweak.

If you have never tried shirataki rice, this will make you a fan. All the comfort, none of the carbs.

Garlicky Lemon Creamed Chicken

Prep: 10 mins | Cook: 5 hours + 5 mins | Total: 5 hours + 15 mins | Serves 4

8 skin-on, bone-in skin-on chicken thighs

Sea salt and ground black pepper

4 fl oz. / ½ cup chicken stock

6 cloves garlic, minced

Zest and juice from 1 large lemon

4 fl oz. / ½ cup heavy cream (double cream) *[For dairy-free sub with thick coconut milk]*

½ tsp. konjac flour / glucomannan powder

Sprinkle sea salt and ground black pepper on the skin of the chicken thighs and then put them **skin side down** in a pan over high heat. You're not trying to cook the chicken, you're only crisping and browning that gorgeous skin, so fast and furious in the frying pan is what we need. You do not need to turn and cook the other side. This will only take a few minutes.

Once the skin is golden and crisp, use tongs and carefully place the chicken pieces **skin side up** in a single layer in your crockpot.

Pour the stock over the chicken, add the minced garlic, cover and cook on low for 5 hours.

Carefully remove the chicken pieces from the crockpot and place in a serving dish, skin side up.

Add the lemon zest, lemon juice, and cream to the juices in the crockpot and whisk together. While still whisking with one hand, gently sprinkle the konjac flour on the surface and whisk in.

Once thickened, pour the lemon garlic sauce over the chicken pieces and serve.

~~~~~~

Top Tip: Go gently and slowly when adding the konjac flour otherwise you will end up with a clumpy sauce. Not one clumpy sauce in sight! Yay!

It's good to remember when coming to a KETO / low-carb way of eating that you get to eat the fattier pieces of the bird – and the skin. Oh, the skin! No more dry, skinless chicken breasts for you! Enjoy all the crispy, fatty, tasty goodness that only the skin gives you.

For more chicken recipes, head to our growing collection over at The Ketovangelist Kitchen:

http://www.ketovangelistkitchen.com/category/chicken-turkey/

The Roast Chicken with Wild Mushroom Sauce is fantastic!

Notato Gratin

Prep: 15 mins | Cook: 7 hours + 5 mins | Total: 7 hours + 20 mins | Serves 8 - 10

1 lb. / 450g turnip

1 lb. / 450g radishes

8 oz. / 225g celeriac (celery root)

4 fl oz. / ½ cup heavy cream (double cream)

Sea salt and ground black pepper

1 TBSP white wine vinegar

2 tsp. dried parsley

1 ½ pints / 3 cups chicken stock

3 tsp. konjac flour / glucomannan powder

6 oz. / 170g Cheddar cheese, shredded

2 oz. / 55g parmesan cheese, finely grated

4 oz. / 110g onions, finely chopped

Peel and thinly slice the turnip, celeriac (celery root), and radishes. If you don't want to peel the radishes just be aware that your Notato Gratin will have a decidedly pink hue to it (don't ask me how I know). If you don't mind that, feel free to just slice those puppies and call it good.

In a large pan over medium heat, mix the cream, sea salt and ground black pepper, white wine vinegar, dried parsley, and chicken stock. As you stir, gently sprinkle the konjac flour over the surface of the liquid and stir well. Add the shredded Cheddar, the grated parmesan, and the finely chopped onions and stir until all the cheeses have melted.

Mix up the sliced veggies and spread one third of them in the bottom of the crockpot. Pour one third of the sauce over the top. Repeat the layers twice more, finishing with a sauce layer.

Put the lid on the crockpot, set to low and cook for 7 hours.

Spoon the Notato Gratin into a serving dish, and sprinkle shredded Cheddar and some chopped onions on top. Place under a hot broiler (grill) for 5 minutes until the cheese and onions are golden brown and bubbling. Watch it carefully! And just say no to burnt gratin.

~~~~~~

Top tip: if your gratin is thicker or thinner than you prefer, see instructions on page 6 to tweak.

Fulfil your potato craving with this Notato Gratin! All the flavor, way less starch. #WINNING

www.carriebrown.com

BBQ Sauce

Prep: 10 mins | Cook: 45 mins | Total: 55 mins | Serves: 2 pints / 1 quart

2 TBSP coconut oil or avocado oil

6 oz. / 170 g onion, diced

2 large cloves garlic, finely chopped

28 oz. / 785 g can diced or crushed tomatoes (unsweetened)

2 TBSP coconut aminos

1 1/2 TBSP apple cider vinegar

3 oz. / 85 g xylitol or erythritol

1 1/2 TBSP lemon juice

2 tsp. smoked paprika

1 tsp. sea salt

1 1/2 tsp. liquid smoke

1/2 tsp. root beer extract

1/2 tsp. konjac flour / glucomannan powder

Heat the oil in a pan. Add the onion and garlic and sauté until translucent – about 5 minutes.

Add the tomatoes, coconut aminos, apple cider vinegar, xylitol, lemon juice, smoked paprika, salt, liquid smoke, and root beer extract, and stir well.

Bring to the boil, reduce heat to low, and simmer for 40 minutes.

Remove the pan from the heat and carefully transfer the sauce into a blender. Blend on high until sauce is completely smooth. Tap the konjac flour through the hole in the top of the blender lid and blend for 5 seconds.

Pour the sauce into a jar and leave uncovered until cool. Cover and refrigerate.

~~~~~~

"Prepare your taste buds for an amazing keto experience! Ribs, chicken, beef, oh my! The flavor of this sauce, caramelized, is out of this world! I've been waiting so long for a BBQ sauce recipe like this!" ~ Lisa

"WOW!! This is really good!!!" ~ Erik

Nicer Than Rice Pudding

Prep: 5 mins | Cook: 6 hours | Total: 6 hours + 5 mins | Serves 8 - 10

1 lb. / 450g riced cauliflower

1 lb. / 450g shirataki rice, rinsed and drained well

8 fl oz. / 1 cup heavy cream (double cream) *[For dairy-free sub thick coconut milk]*

8 fl oz. / 1 cup water

2 oz. / 55g butter, melted *[For dairy-free omit]*

5 TBSP maple extract

7 TBSP xylitol or erythritol

1 tsp. konjac flour / glucomannan powder

4 oz. pecans, chopped and toasted

Place riced cauliflower, rinsed and drained shirataki rice, cream, water, melted butter, maple extract, xylitol or erythritol in the crockpot and stir well.

While stirring the mixture with one hand, sprinkle the konjac flour gently over the surface and mix well.

Put the lid on the crockpot, set to low and cook for 6 hours.

Remove the lid from the crockpot and stir in the chopped, toasted pecans.

Spoon into bowls and serve with heavy cream (double cream).

~~~~~~

Top Tip: Go gently and slowly when adding the konjac flour otherwise you will end up with a clumpy pudding. Who wants clumpy pudding? Exactly no one.

Top tip: if your pudding is thicker or thinner than you prefer, see instructions on page 6 to tweak, using water and not stock (obviously). You could also use almond milk.

I made this for Alisen, after one of our weekly, Sunday morning visits to sit by the open fire in our local coffee shop. We were brainstorming on various food ideas and she suddenly said, "You need to make Rice Pudding". And thus, because I love Alisen very much, the very next weekend instead of going to the coffee shop she came over to hang in my kitchen and I had a crockpot full of this ready for her to taste test. We poured cream, drank coffee, and we ooohed and ahhhed.

We thought it was like a cross between rice pudding and porridge (oatmeal). So eat it in the morning instead of oatmeal, or as dessert instead of rice pudding. Either way, it is The Bomb.

Strawberry Surprise Crumble

Prep: 10 mins | Cook: 2 hours + 10 mins | Total: 2 hours + 20 mins | Serves 8 - 10

3 oz. / 85g butter

3 oz. / 85g erythritol

1 lb. radishes, cut in half and thinly sliced into semi-circles

1 tsp. vanilla extract

2 lb. frozen strawberries, defrosted with their juice

3 tsp. konjac flour / glucomannan powder

coconut or avocado oil spray

4 oz. almond flour

4 oz. erythritol (DO NOT SUB with another sweetener!)

1 tsp. baking powder

3 oz. sliced almonds

½ tsp. sea salt

¾ oz. coconut flour

3 oz. butter, melted

1 TBSP erythritol (DO NOT SUB with another sweetener!)

Heat the butter and erythritol together over a medium heat and stir to combine until melted. It will get very hot, be careful of splatters! It may also steam. Don't panic! But do be careful.

Add the radish slices to the hot butter in the pan and sauté the radishes for a few minutes until they become translucent. The butter / erythritol mixture is extremely hot, so this will not take very long. Be very careful not to splash or touch the mixture. Once the radishes are translucent, remove the pan from the heat and add the vanilla extract and the defrosted strawberries and their juice, and mix. While stirring with one hand, gently sprinkle the konjac flour over the surface and stir well.

Spray the crockpot with coconut or avocado oil and spread the strawberry mixture evenly in the bottom. Leave to cool so that the strawberry mixture thickens.

Place the almond flour, erythritol, baking powder, sliced almonds, sea salt and coconut flour in a bowl and mix together well. Pour in the melted butter and stir until you have a crumble with the butter evenly coating everything.

Spoon the crumble over the strawberry mixture in the crockpot and spread it evenly to completely cover the filling.

If you are using a traditional crockpot, place a clean dish towel (tea towel) over top of the crockpot container before putting the lid on. This helps enormously to reduce excess water from building up inside the crockpot and giving you a watery dish. If you are using an Instant Pot on the crockpot setting, make sure that the pressure valve on top of the lid is set to "vent", for the same reason. This is especially important for this recipe, otherwise you run the risk of having a soggy crumble, and no one wants soggy crumble. If you don't want to use a dish towel, you can also use several (and by several I mean like 10) thicknesses of paper towels.

Place the lid on top of the dish towel or paper towels and lock the lid in place. Again, if you're using an Instant Pot, be sure to check that the pressure valve on the top of the lid is switched to "vent".

Turn the crockpot on high for 2 hours. Remove the lid and sprinkle the remaining tablespoon of erythritol evenly over the surface of the crumble.

Carefully remove the crockpot container from the base, place on a baking sheet, and put under a hot broiler (grill) for 5 minutes until the crumble is golden brown and crisp. Watch it carefully!

Carefully remove the crumble from the oven and leave to rest for 20 minutes. It will be volcanically hot for quite a while afterwards, so don't worry about it getting cold. The crumble will also crisp up as it cools down.

Spoon into dishes and serve with whipped heavy cream (double cream).

Note: your crumble will look different because my photo is of version 1, while the recipe is for version 2, which is better ☺

~~~~~~

Top Tip: make the strawberry mixture ahead and store in the 'fridge. Remove from the 'fridge the day you are cooking the crumble and allow to warm before putting in the crockpot container.

I can't tell you how entirely thrilled I am that I was able to get a crumble out of a crockpot and it not be a soggy mess. And the fact that it's a low-carb KETO crumble almost made me weep with joy. But there's more: even after 4 days in the 'fridge that crumble DOES NOT GO SOGGY.

Also, no, you cannot taste the radishes. NO ONE believed it had radishes in when I gave it to them. You won't either. Even after I told them and they went poking around in the crumble they didn't believe me. The flavor is all strawberries all the time, but with less carbs. Because radishes. BOOM.

 "The strawberry crumble is like eating strawberry rhubarb pie with an impossibly crispy, nutty topping - berry deliciousness!" ~ Sara

"What a fun recipe! I love this delicious result of Carrie's creative cooking style. Just wait, you won't believe her ingredients list. An amazing desert the entire family will enjoy." ~ Minta

KETOVANGELIST KITCHEN RESOURCES

WEBSITE : www.ketovangelistkitchen.com

PODCAST : www.ketovangelistkitchen.com/category/podcast

FACEBOOK GROUP : www.facebook.com/groups/ketovangelistkitchen

TWITTER : www.twitter.com/KetovanKitchen

PINTEREST : www.pinterest.com/KetovanKitchen

INSTAGRAM : www.instagram.com/ketovangelistkitchen

KETOVANGELIST GENERAL KETO RESOURCES

WEBSITE : www.ketovangelistkitchen.com

PODCAST : www.ketovangelist.com/category/podcast/

FACEBOOK GROUP : www.facebook.com/groups/theketogenicathlete/

KETOGENIC ATHLETE RESOURCES

WEBSITE : www.theketogenicathlete.com

PODCAST : www.theketogenicathlete.com/category/podcast/

FACEBOOK GROUP : www.facebook.com/groups/theketogenicathlete/

WHERE TO FIND ME

www.CarrieBrown.com : delicious recipes for optimal nutrition, wellness, & fat-loss, with tips & tricks for living a super healthy, sane life, as well as travel & things to make you think.

PODCAST : www.ketovangelistkitchen.com/category/podcast

FACEBOOK (page) : www.facebook.com/CarrieBrownBlog

FACEBOOK (personal) : www.facebook.com/flamingavocado

TWITTER : www.twitter.com/CarrieBrownBlog

PINTEREST : www.pinterest.com/CarrieBrownBlog

INSTAGRAM
@carrieontrippin : day-to-day moments captured with my iPhone
@biggirlcamera : road trips, landscapes, flowers, fences, barns, & whatever else grabs my attention captured with my Big Girl Camera
@lifeinthesanelane : food, recipes, inspiration, and sane living tips
@mistermchenry : The world according to Mr. McHenry

FLICKR : www.flickr.com/photos/carrieontrippin

MEDIUM : www.medium.com/@CarrieBrownBlog : random musings on life, the Universe, & everything. Possibly rantier, more sensitive, & more controversial.

COOKBOOKS

E-cookbook / pdf versions : www.carriebrown.com/archives/31768

Print versions : www.amazon.com/author/browncarrie

I am an author, podcast co-host, recipe developer, & photographer, creating useful, fun, & beautiful stuff about food, travel, and living a sane life.

I use my ex-professional pastry chef talents to create scrumptious recipes to help the world eat smarter, live better, & put the 'healthy' back into healthy again. I create gluten-free, grain-free, sugar-free recipes for LCHF, KETO, SANE, LowCarb, Paleo, Primal, WheatBelly, Wild Diet, & other health-focused dietary approaches.

This cookbook joins the "Eat Smarter!" series of cookbooks which includes Ice creams, Smoothies and Sides, Soups, Beverages, and Holidays, on the culinary bookshelf. All jammed with serious whole food, low-carb goodness & YUM.

When I am not making stuff up in the kitchen you'll likely find me roaring around the country shooting landscapes & otherwise exploring this amazing world that we live in. I like life better when it's real, rambunctious, & slightly irreverent.

I resolved my BiPolar II disorder, have an accent like crack (apparently), & a love for people who keep on going when the going gets tough. I think leeks are the finest vegetables on earth, and I have a huge soft spot for pork belly. I can't swim.

I love living in Seattle with a couple of large cameras, a ridiculous amount of cocoa powder, & a pile of cats — Florence, Zebedee, Daisy, & Mr. McHenry. We love it here!

PORK (*dairy-free)

Carnitas Omelet..21*

Carnival Sausages..25*

Cheesy Sausage Hodgepodge..27

Lemon Pepper Cream Pork Chops..23

Pork and Fennel Hash..17*

Pork Chops with Herby Leek Sauce..13*

Sage & Bacon Pork with Bacon Cream Sauce............................11*

Sausage Hash Pie..15

Sour Cream BBQ Pulled Pork..19*

BEEF (*dairy-free)

BBQ Pulled Beef..37*

BBQ Pulled Beef Tacos..39*

Beef Pot Roast..35*

Beefcake Stew..43*

Boozy Braised Beef Short Ribs..33*

Mighty Meat Pizza..45

Sour Cream Mushroom Short Ribs..47

Shredded Balsamic Beef..29*

Shredded Balsamic Beef Boats..31*

We Don't Need No Beans Chili..41*

SEAFOOD

Clam Chowder..49

CHICKEN (*dairy-free)

SIDE DISHES (*dairy-free)

DESSERTS (*dairy-free)

45888720R00059

Made in the USA
Middletown, DE
16 July 2017